This book belongs to:

______________________________

# DISCOVER the STORY of Captain Kate McCue

with Bearific®

KATELYN LONAS

# Table of Contents


Introduction........................1
Early Life..........................2
Education...........................5
Career..............................8
Achievement........................13
Pioneer............................16
Essentials.........................19
Wrap Up............................24
Becoming...........................27
Duties.............................30
Advice.............................31
Beyond.............................34
Rescues............................37
Fun Facts..........................44
Pictures...........................47

# Introduction

"This is Captain Kate, but you can call me Captain because it took me 19 years to earn this title."

Discover Captain Kate's journey to becoming the first American woman to Captain a mega cruise ship.

# Early Life

Captain Kate was born on January 6th, 1978, in San Francisco, California.

During her childhood, she traveled a lot with her family due to her father's employment as an engineer and they have spent time living in Michigan and Evans, Georgia.

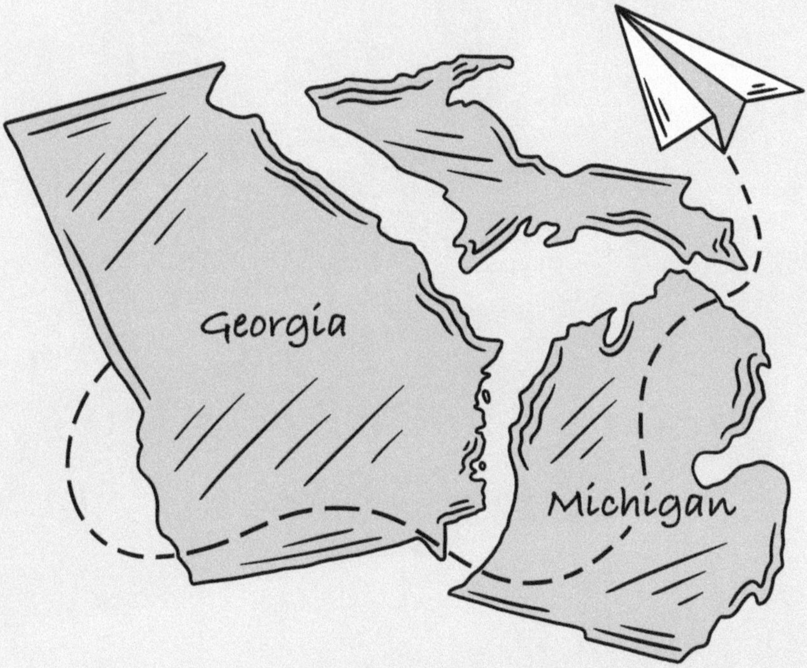


Captain Kate's interest in sailing began when she was twelve. Over Thanksgiving, she went on a four-day cruise to the Bahamas with her parents and brother.

After their trip, she told her father how she wants to be a Cruise Director when she grows up.

Her dad responded and told her, "You can do anything you want, including drive the thing."

This was the beginning of Captain Kate's journey.

# Education

Captain Kate attended Lakeside High School.

After that, she enrolled at the California Maritime Academy in 1996, where she graduated in 2000 with a bachelor's degree in business administration.

During summer breaks Captain Kate went on sailing trips and studied celestial navigation.

Celestial navigation is used to calculate position by utilizing the moon, stars, sun, and horizon.

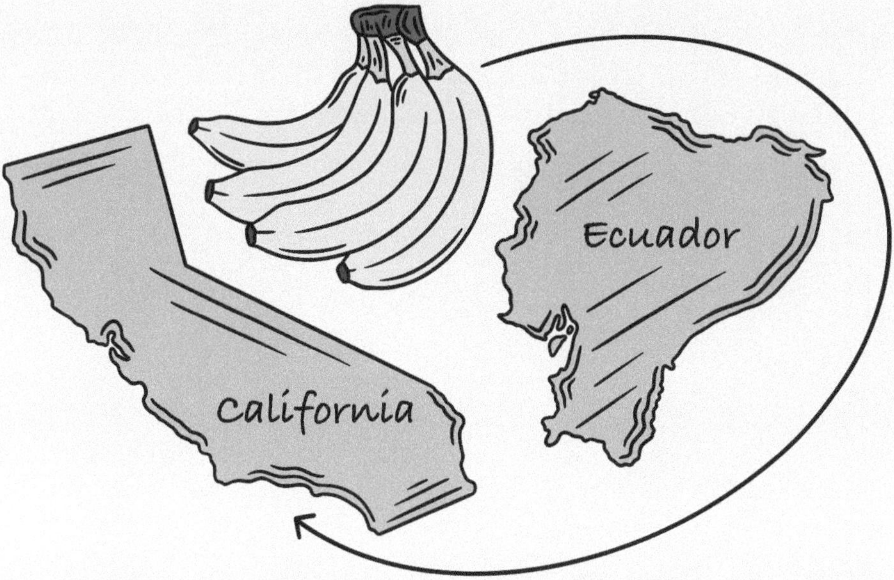


While pursuing her degree, Captain Kate completed an internship with Chiquita Brands International, working on one of their cargo ships that transported bananas from Ecuador to Long Beach, California.

# Career

After receiving her degree, Captain Kate traveled to Maui in the Hawaiian Islands and lived with her cousins for six months while working as a general deck hand on a catamaran that took tourists on cruises to the Molokini Crater.

Later, Captain Kate joined Maersk Sealand in Los Angeles as a logistics manager, although she still desired to work at sea.

After nine months of submitting applications to several cruise lines with no response, she applied to be a bartender at Disney.

However, Captain Kate was overqualified for this position, so they passed on her resume, and she landed a job as a Third Mate with Disney Cruise Line.

During this time, Disney only had two cruise ships, and there wasn't very much room for growth.

Therefore, in 2003, Captain Kate became a Second Officer for the Royal Caribbean Cruise, and just after one year, she was promoted to First Officer.

In 2009, Captain Kate attended the Maritime Institute of Technology and Graduate Studies, where she received her Chief Mate and Master's License, which allow her to be in charge or in command of a vessel.

Captain Kate later returned to the Royal Caribbean Cruise and was appointed Chief Officer, then Staff Captain, in 2011.

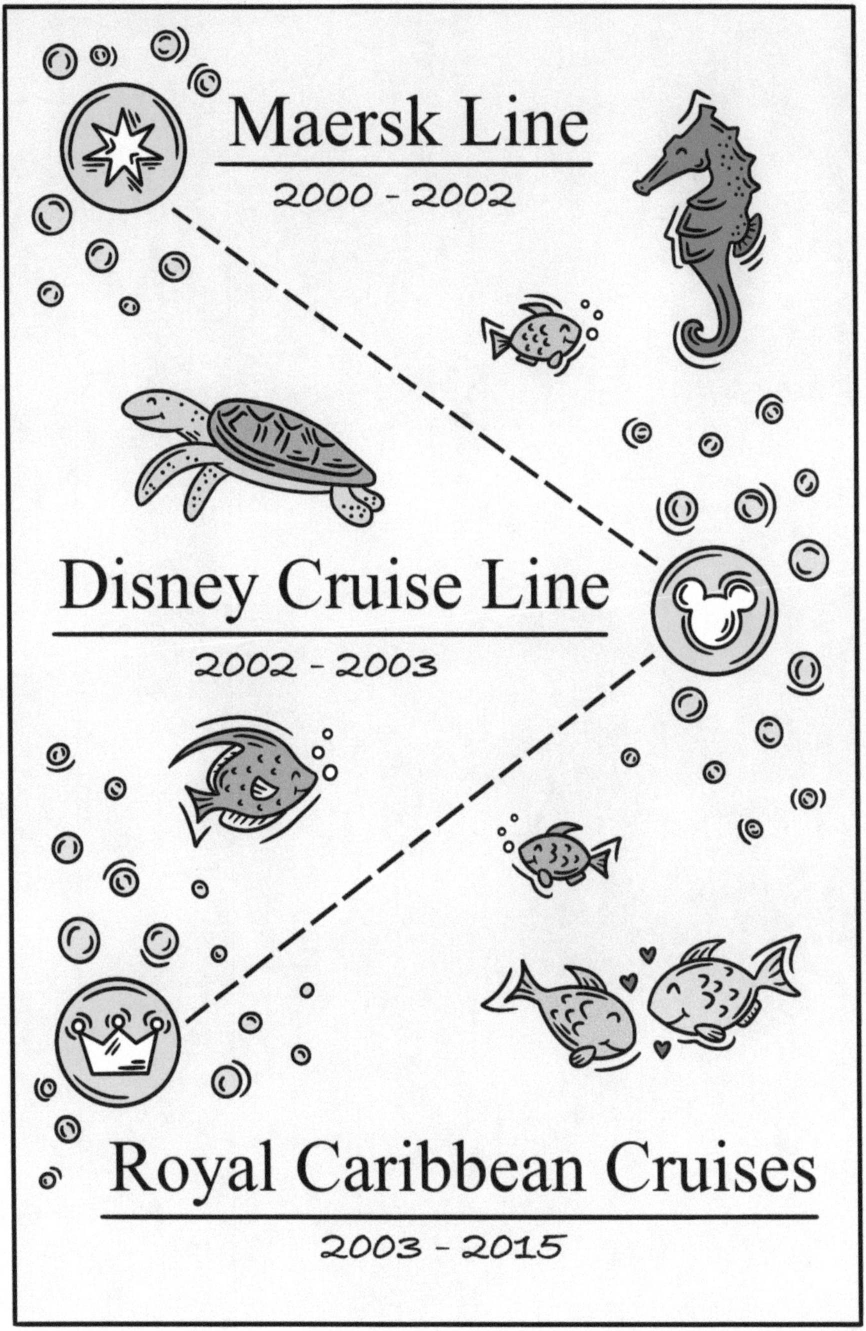
Maersk Line
2000 - 2002
Disney Cruise Line
2002 - 2003
Royal Caribbean Cruises
2003 - 2015

# Achievement

In 2015, Captain Kate was contacted by the President of Celebrity Cruises, Lisa Lutoff-Perlo, to apply for the position of Captain.

Captain Kate applied for the role and made history on September 13, 2015, by becoming the first American woman to Captain a mega cruise ship.

Captain Kate achieved her dream after 19 years of hard work, determination, focus, dedication, and passion.

This shows everyone in the world that you can do anything you dream of as long as you believe in yourself and never give up.

Captain Kate started as Commanding Officer of the Celebrity Summit.

In 2018, she became the Commanding Officer on Celebrity Equinox.

In 2019, she became the Commanding Officer on Celebrity Edge.

Since 2022, she has been the Captain of the newest 1.3 billion-dollar cruise ship, Celebrity Beyond.

# Pioneer

Captain Kate broke the gender barrier and inspired people around the world to reach for their goals.

She is currently sharing her experience with others online and has amassed over 4 million followers across multiple social media platforms.

The Celebrity Cruises President, Lisa Lutoff-Perlo, has also publicly stated that,

"This is a day that I've been waiting for since we made the first cut of steel on our beautiful Celebrity Beyond. Captain Kate has transcended what it means to be a captain as a voice and example of inclusivity, diversity, and change."

Media outlets such as Fortune, USA Today, Wall Street Journal, New York Times, Los Angeles Times, and many other publications have written articles and conducted interviews about Captain Kate and her remarkable career.

# Essentials

Captain Kate brings three essential items onboard the Celebrity Beyond.

These items include her mermaid tail, black platform Christian Louboutin heels with red soles, and Bug Naked, her sphynx cat.

Captain Kate's favorite hobby is to explore the sea and go on adventures in her mermaid tail.

She enjoys wearing her mermaid tail to swim in the Celebrity Beyond pool and in the ocean while the ship is docked at port.

Captain Kate always travels with her Louboutin heels.

This pair of heels holds sentimental value because it was the one item she purchased to celebrate her promotion to Captain.

Bug Naked is Captain Kate's #1 sidekick and has been sailing the sea since she was three months old.

Bug Naked is an elf-eared sphynx cat with beautiful aqua eyes. Her name was inspired by "Love Bug," which was Captain Kate's nickname growing up.

Bug Naked was born on March 20, 2016, and has always brought good luck onboard the ship.

Currently, Bug has over a hundred outfits, uniforms, and costumes.

Every week on the Celebrity Beyond, there is a game called "Bug Trivia" and the winner of this game is awarded with a limited edition collector Bug pin as well as a snuggle with Bug.

# Wrap Up

Las Vegas

As of today, Captain Kate lives in Las Vegas, Nevada, with her husband, Nikola Petrovic, who is also in the cruising industry.

They met in 2006 while working onboard a Royal Caribbean Cruise.

Currently, Captain Kate works every three months as the Commanding Officer of the Celebrity Beyond Ship.

Captain Kate has taken thousands of passengers across the world to explore different destinations. One of the many voyages she has taken cruise ship guests on is the European Cruise.

The European Cruise is a ten-night round trip where you get to visit countries such as Italy, Greece, Montenegro, and Croatia.

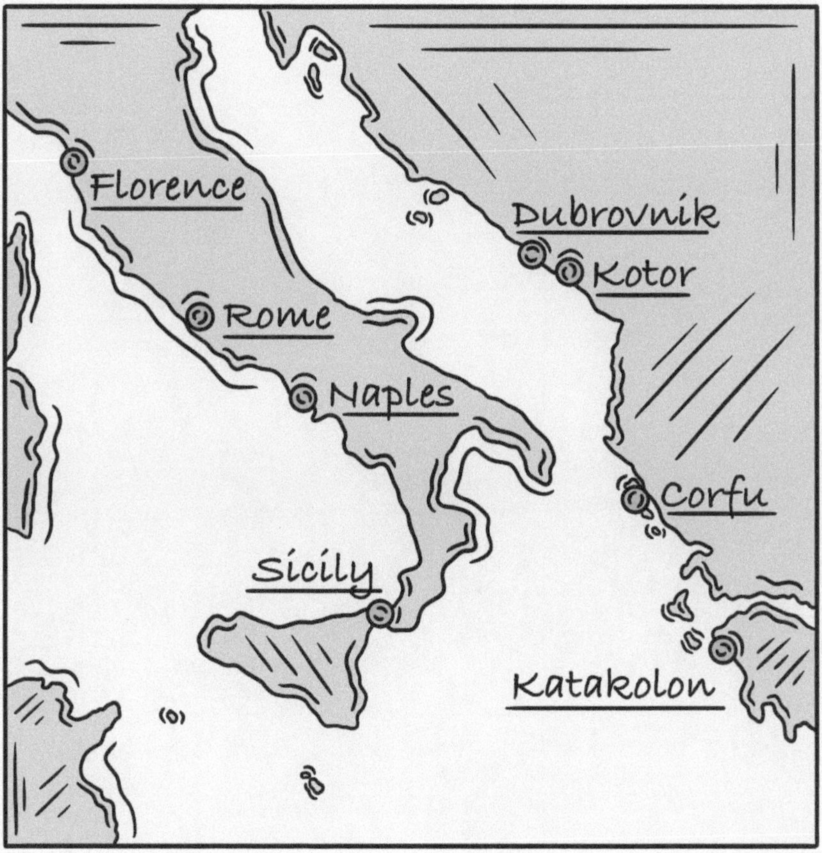

# Becoming

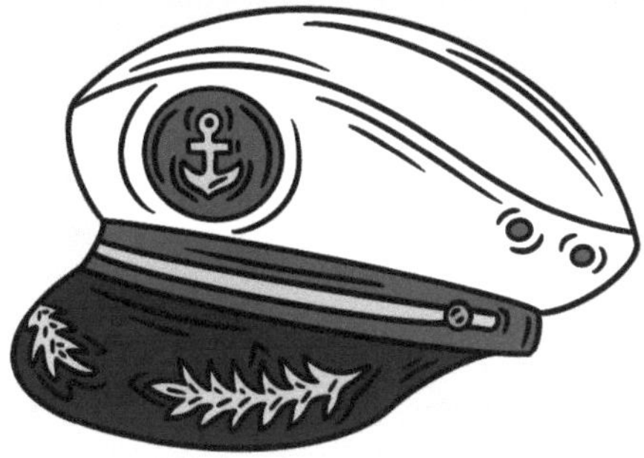

Many people may wonder: How do you become a Cruise Ship Captain?

According to Captain Kate, it's important to remember that "good things come to those who put in the time and effort." Becoming a

Cruise Ship Captain is a marathon, not a sprint.

It is not an easy path to becoming a Ship Captain. Before you take the final exam for your license, you must have completed several years of education, earned good grades, and gained lots of experience. After graduation, you'll need to work your way up and spend a lot of time at sea.

Have a highschool diploma.

(or something equivalent)

Earn a postsecondary degree.

(a bachelor's or master's degree )

Gain experience.

(can start as a third mate )

Obtain the necessary licenses.

(attend a Maritime Academy)

Work your way up.

(Chief Officer & Staff Captain)

CAPTAIN

(apply for position)

# Duties

The Captain of a ship is responsible for the crew members' and passengers' safety and well-being.

The Commanding Officer is also in charge of the cruise ship's safe and efficient operation and management.

# Advice

Some advice from Captain Kate for success in any industry or career is:

"Understanding who you are as a person, your priorities, and knowing what you want is key.  Surround yourself with diversity; be your authentic self, approachable, and vulnerable. Be kind, be supportive, and pay it forward."

"You don't need to follow in anyone else's footsteps. Forge your own path by bringing your unique personality and perspective to each job you do."

# Captain Kate's favorite words of wisdom:

"Never put yourself in a position to lose."
- CMA President, Captain Jerry Aspland

"Have gratitude, not attitude."
- Captain Kate

"Stop waiting for the light at the end of the tunnel. Just light it yourself."
- Captain Kate's Mum

# Beyond

Celebrity Beyond is the third ship in the Celebrity Cruises Edge Series.

This cruise ship was built by Chantiers de l'Atlantique and launched in April 2022. Beyond can accommodate up to 5,303 people.

Currently, the Celebrity Beyond Ship has won three awards, such as the 2022 Gold Award Spa Design, the 2022 Gold Award Premium Ship, and the 2022 Silver Award Cusine.

Celebrity Beyond offers 32 distinct restaurants, bars, cafes, and lounges.

They also provide a variety of entertainment options in the theater, casino, resort, bars, and shops.

| | |
|---|---|
| Passengers<br>3,260 | Tonnage<br>141,420 |
| Length<br>1,073 ft | Beam<br>128 ft |
| Draught<br>27 ft | Speed<br>22 kts |

# Rescues

As of today, Captain Kate and her crew have rescued three boats lost at sea.

Captain Kate was in charge of the Celebrity Summit, and on December 16, 2017, she received a mayday call from a boat in distress.

Captain Kate and her crew, without hesitation, headed straight to the boat to assist.

What they discovered was a sailboat sinking with three men and three women onboard. Two of these women were also pregnant.

They lowered the tender and sent security and medical teams to retrieve them.

These survivors drifted for over a month at sea without

a sail, and they had no food for the last six days.

In the end, all of them were saved thanks to the efforts of Captain Kate and her crew.

On January 2, 2023, onboard Celebrity Beyond, Captain Kate was informed by her Chief Officer that there was a boat full of people who appeared to be in distress.

Captain Kate maneuvered the cruise ship so they could bring in the boat safely.

Once the boat was secured, the crew members quickly jumped into action and provided the people with warm blankets, new clothes, food, a medical evaluation, and a chance to call home.

Thanks to Captain Kate and the Celebrity Beyond crew, nineteen people were able to see the rest of 2023.

On August 30, 2023, onboard Celebrity Beyond, Captain Kate and her crew received a call on VHF channel 16 from an Italian Coast Guard vessel regarding an ongoing search and rescue operation.

The Italian Coast Guard requested that Celebrity Beyond approach their position to create shelter from the wind and sea so they can help the fishing boat in distress.

The Celebrity Beyond crew prepared extra life jackets after being informed that more than two hundred people were onboard the fishing vessel.

Another Coast Guard arrived to assist with the scene, and all of the people onboard the fishing vessel were saved.

These rescues at sea are Captain Kate's proudest moments in her career.

When it comes to rescuing life at sea, the International Convention for Safety of Life at Sea provides guidance and states that:

"The master of a ship at sea, on receiving a signal from any source that a ship, aircraft, or survival craft thereof is in distress, is bound to proceed with all speed to the assistance of the persons in distress, informing them if possible that he is doing so."

# Fun Facts

Ship Captains have the authority to perform legal marriage ceremonies onboard their vessels.

Cats have long been thought to bring good luck on ships. Many British and Irish sailors chose cats to accompany them on their sailing adventures. This belief was also held by Vikings in Northern Germany between the 8th and 11th centuries.

Whistling aboard a boat is considered unlucky among sailors since it is believed to bring strong winds.

Bananas aboard a ship are thought to bring trouble out in the open sea. This belief is based on the fact that ships carrying bananas from the Caribbean to Spain frequently went missing in the 18th century.

A knot is a nautical measurement that originates from the olden days when ships assessed their speed by tossing a log fastened to a rope with evenly spaced knots into the water. The number of knots would be counted during a certain period of time to determine the ship's speed as it moved.

# Pictures

Captain Kate onboard Celebrity Beyond with Bug Naked.

Captain Kate and her husband.

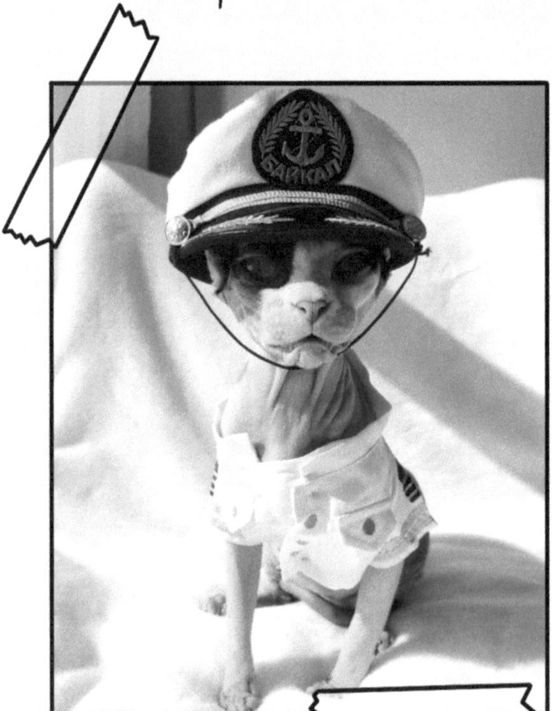

Bug in her
Captain outfit.

Captain Kate having fun bartending onboard Celebrity Beyond.

Captain Kate in the sea.

Captain Kate in the Celebrity Beyond pool.

Captain Kate with the Celebrity Beyond Cruise.

More of Captain Kate can be found on social media platforms such as Instagram, TikTok, and YouTube. @captainkatemccue

Captain Kate's website: www.thecaptainkate.com

"If you can sea it,
you can be it."

- Captain Kate McCue -

# The End!

*remember to:*

BELIEVE
DREAM
ACHIEVE

More Bearific® books on bearific.com

*Author & Illustrator*

# Katelyn Lonas

Katelyn is 17 years old and resides in Southern California. Katelyn loves to encourage others to always believe in themselves and chase after their dreams! She began writing and illustrating her first book at age 9 and went on to publish 67 more books. She hopes you enjoyed this book and are excited for more to come!

- Katelyn Lonas

Printed in the USA
CPSIA information can be obtained
at www.ICGtesting.com
LVHW061029290424
778755LV00001B/1
* 9 7 8 1 9 5 5 0 1 3 9 0 1 *